Sheep

ABDO
Publishing Company

A Buddy Book
by
Julie Murray

VISIT US AT

www.abdopub.com

Published by Buddy Books, an imprint of ABDO Publishing Company, 4940 Viking Drive, Suite 622, Edina, Minnesota 55435. Copyright © 2005 by Abdo Consulting Group, Inc. International copyrights reserved in all countries. No part of this book may be reproduced in any form without written permission from the publisher.

Printed in the United States.

Edited by: Christy DeVillier
Contributing Editors: Matt Ray, Michael P. Goecke
Graphic Design: Maria Hosley
Image Research: Deborah Coldiron
Photographs: Corbis, Photodisc, Photoessentials

Library of Congress Cataloging-in-Publication Data

Murray, Julie, 1969-
  Sheep/Julie Murray.
      p. cm. — (Animal kingdom. Set II)
  Includes bibliographical references and index.
  Contents: Sheep — Different breeds — Size, coat, and color — Their bodies — What do sheep eat? — Where do sheep live? — Babies — Sheep uses — Sheep facts.
  ISBN 1-59197-335-X
    1. Sheep—Juvenile literature. [1. Sheep.] I. Title.

SF375.2.M86 2003
636.3—dc21

2003042583

Contents

Sheep

People kept sheep as long as 6,000 years ago. The person who watched over sheep was called a shepherd. Back then, people used sheep to carry heavy loads. They drank the sheep's milk. Long ago, people made yarn from sheep wool, too.

Today, farmers raise sheep in many parts of the world. Sheep are important for wool, meat, and leather.

Many sheep today live on farms or ranches.

What They Look Like

Rams are male sheep. Ewes are female sheep. Rams grow bigger than ewes. Adult rams weigh between 150 and 400 pounds (68 and 181 kg).

Sheep have a thick coat of hair. This hair is called wool or fleece. Sheep fleece may be white, tan, brown, or black.

Fleece is a sheep's wool coat.

Some kinds of sheep grow horns. A **ewe's** horns are small and sharp. Some **rams** grow big, curled horns.

Sheep have two toes on each foot. Each toe has a hard covering called a hoof. Hoofs help sheep climb in steep and rocky places.

This ram has curled horns.

Where They Live

Many sheep live on farms. There are sheep farms in many parts of the world. China and Australia have the most sheep farms.

Farm sheep live outside most of the year. Their **fleece** coat keeps them warm and dry.

These merino sheep
live in Australia.

Wild sheep live in Asia, Europe, and North America. They live in deserts, fields, or mountains. North America has bighorn sheep and thinhorn sheep. Bighorn sheep have bigger horns.

Bighorn sheep live in North America.

Kinds Of Sheep

There are more than 800 kinds of sheep. Merino sheep are raised for their fine wool. Farmers cut off, or **shear**, the sheep's wool and sell it.

Suffolk sheep are raised for their meat. People around the world eat sheep meat. Meat from an adult sheep is called **mutton**.

These people are shearing sheep.

People buy sheep fleece to make wool yarn.

Roquefort sheep are raised for their milk. People use the milk to make Roquefort cheese.

Sheep Wool

One sheep can grow eight pounds (four kg) of wool in a year. One pound (454 g) of sheep wool can make 10 miles (16 km) of yarn.

Wool is warm and lasts a long time. People make sweaters, socks, and mittens with wool. Rugs, blankets, and many other things have wool, too.

Eating

Sheep spend many hours each day eating. They eat grass and hay. Some farm sheep eat grain, too. Wild sheep also eat shrubs. Sheep can eat between two and four pounds (one and two kg) each day.

Sheep chew their cud.

Sheep are **ruminants**. Ruminants have a special way of breaking up food. Food goes down to one part of a sheep's four-part stomach. Later, this food comes back up to the sheep's mouth. It will chew this food, or cud, and swallow again. And then, the other stomach parts will finish breaking up the cud.

Lambs

Young sheep are called **lambs**.
Ewes commonly have one or two
lambs at a time. A newborn lamb
weighs about nine pounds (four kg). It
can stand up and drink its mother's milk
right away.

Lambs are young sheep.

This lamb is drinking its mother's milk.

Lambs run around and play with other lambs. It takes a year for them to become adult sheep. Sheep can live as long as 13 years.

Lambs resting in the grass.

Important Words

ewe a female sheep.

fleece a sheep's wool coat.

lamb a young sheep.

mutton meat from an adult sheep.

ram an adult male sheep.

ruminant an animal that chews its cud. Ruminants have a stomach with three or four parts.

shear to cut off a sheep's fleece.

Web Sites

To learn more about sheep, visit ABDO Publishing Company on the World Wide Web. Web sites about sheep are featured on our Book Links page. These links are routinely monitored and updated to provide the most current information available.

www.abdopub.com

Index

Date Due

HELLERTOWN LIBRARY